FAST!

SUPERCARS

...and other fast machines on the road

QED Publishing

IAN GRAHAM

The words in **bold** are explained in the Glossary on page 30.

Front cover: **The Bugatti Veyron
is one of the world's fastest
supercars (see page 10).**

Editor: Angela Royston
Designer: Andy Crowson
Picture Researcher: Maria Joannou

Copyright © QED Publishing 2010

First published in the UK in 2010 by
QED Publishing
A Quarto Group Company
226 City Road
London EC1V 2TT

www.qed-publishing.co.uk

A catalogue record for this book is available from the British Library.

ISBN 978 1 84835 358 9

Printed in China

Picture credits
Alamy Images Motoring Picture Library 25tl, Rhys Stacker 25tr;
Bloodhound SSC Curventa 29t & c; **Corbis** Transtock 6–7, Car Culture 7c,
George Tiedemann/GT Images 9t, Car Culture 12, Bettmann 16, 17t, 17b, 20,
21b, 22t, 22–23, 23c, Skyscan 27t; **Getty Images** 5bl, 27b, Hulton Archive/
H.F. Davis/Stringer 14, Science & Society Picture Library 15t, Hulton Archive
19b, John Chapple 26–27; **North American Eagle, Inc** Rachel Shadle 28;
Photolibrary National Motor Museum 21t, 23t, 25b; **Rex Features** Sipa
Press 24–25 (background), John Curtis 25tc; **Shelby Supercars** 10, 11t,
11b; **Shutterstock** Gustavo Fadel FC, Christoff 7b, AJancso 8, Renkshot 9b,
Hypnotype BC; **Top 1 Oil Products Company** 13t, 13b; **Topham Picturepoint**
5t, 18t, National Motor Museum/HIP 18b, 19t; **Wikimedia Commons** 4, 5br,
Brian Snelson 7t, Przemysław Jahr 15b

Contents

Note: The cars appear in order of speed, from the slowest to the fastest.

Fastest on wheels

Just over 100 years ago, the fastest cars were slower than a family car today. Now, the world's fastest cars are speedier than a jet airliner.

Never satisfied

One of the oddest record breakers was an **electric car** called *La Jamais Contente*. Its name means 'never satisfied' in French. It was an iron tube with a pointed nose and tail. When scientists saw it, they thought it would go so fast that the driver would not be able to breathe! Luckily, they were wrong. The driver, Camille Jenatzy, set a world record speed of 105 **kilometres** per hour on 29 April 1899, and he lived to tell the tale.

Camille Jenatzy shows off his car,
La Jamais Contente, in 1899.

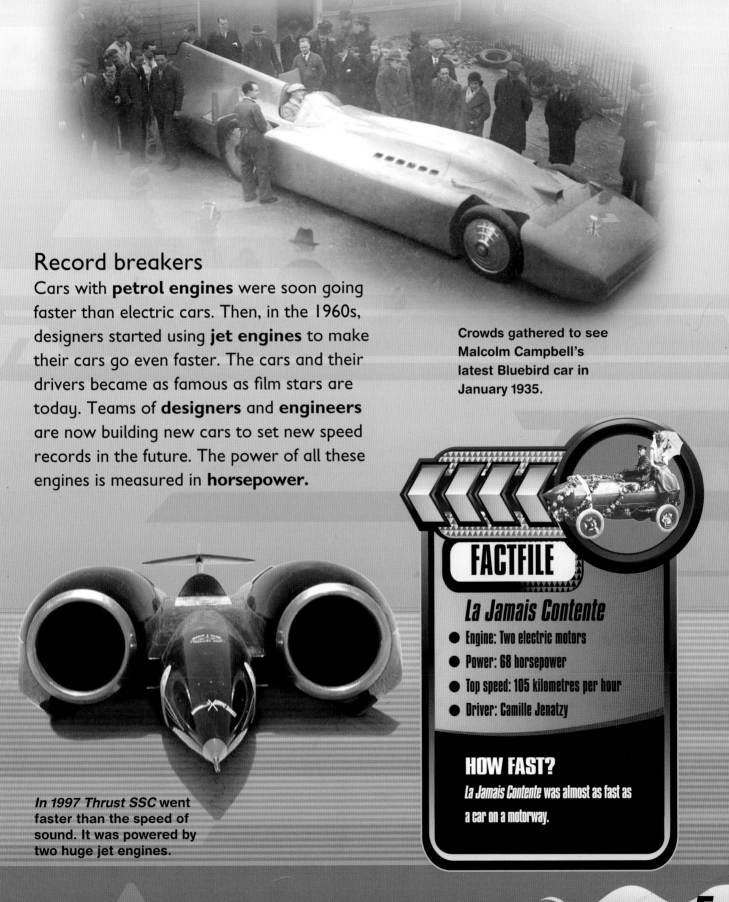

Record breakers

Cars with **petrol engines** were soon going faster than electric cars. Then, in the 1960s, designers started using **jet engines** to make their cars go even faster. The cars and their drivers became as famous as film stars are today. Teams of **designers** and **engineers** are now building new cars to set new speed records in the future. The power of all these engines is measured in **horsepower.**

Crowds gathered to see Malcolm Campbell's latest Bluebird car in January 1935.

In 1997 Thrust SSC went faster than the speed of sound. It was powered by two huge jet engines.

FACTFILE

La Jamais Contente

- Engine: Two electric motors
- Power: 68 horsepower
- Top speed: 105 kilometres per hour
- Driver: Camille Jenatzy

HOW FAST?

La Jamais Contente was almost as fast as a car on a motorway.

Classic cars

Some cars are so successful that they become classics. Classics are still great cars, even when they are out of date.

Classic racing car

The Bugatti Type 35 is probably the most successful racing car ever made. It won up to 2000 races in the 1920s and 1930s. Another Italian car-maker, Ferrari, is one of the most famous names in motor racing. Ferrari also make sports cars for the road.

The Bugatti Type 35 racing car won the Grand Prix world championship of 1926.

Classic sports cars

The Ferrari 250 GTO, a 1960s sports car, is still thought to be one of the best sports cars ever made. An Italian tractor-maker called Ferruccio Lamborghini decided to build his own high-quality fast cars to rival Ferrari. One of his cars, the Lamborghini Diablo, was the fastest road car in the world when it went on sale in 1990.

Only 36 Ferrari 250 GTOs were built to compete in sports car races between 1962 and 1964.

The Lamborghini Diablo's engine is in the middle of the car, behind the driver.

FACTFILE

Lamborghini Diablo

- Engine: 5.7 litres V12
- Power: 492 horsepower
- Top speed: 325 kilometres per hour

HOW FAST?

A Lamborghini Diablo is as fast as a racing car today.

Racing cars

Soon after the first cars were built, people wanted to know which car was the fastest. Cars were soon being built specially for racing.

Open-wheel racers

The top international racing competition is called Formula 1. Racing cars are single-seaters, and are also called open-wheel cars. These cars can reach a top speed of about 380 kilometres per hour. In the USA, the IndyCar series is the most popular competition for open-wheel cars.

Open-wheel racing cars have wings at the front and back to help them go around bends faster.

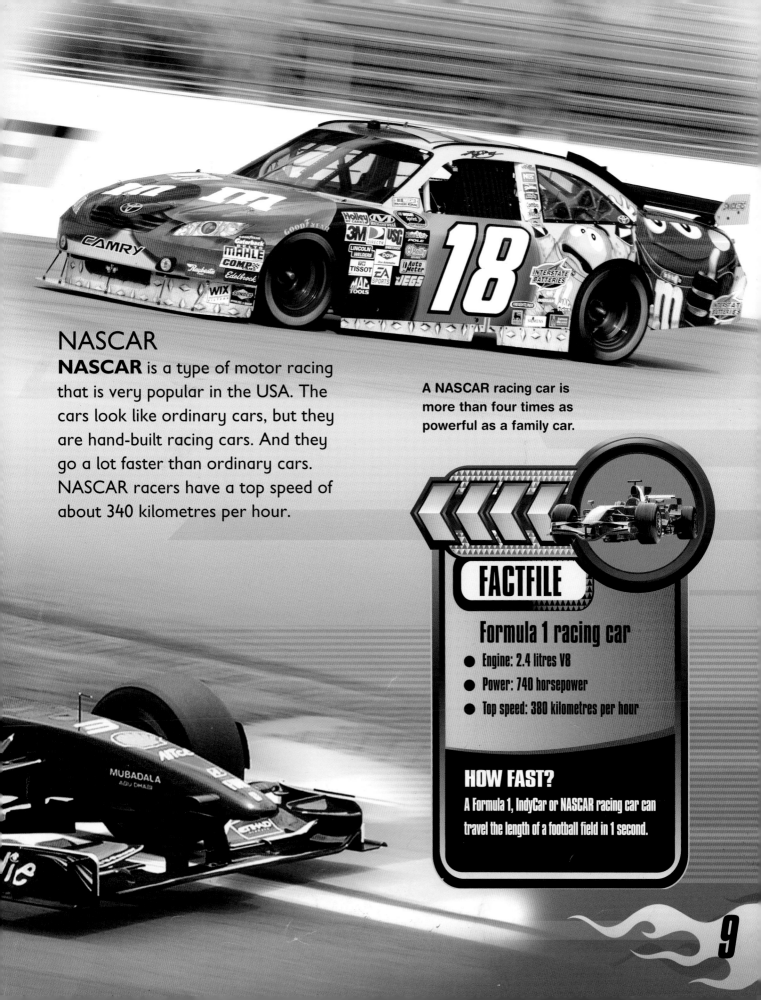

NASCAR

NASCAR is a type of motor racing that is very popular in the USA. The cars look like ordinary cars, but they are hand-built racing cars. And they go a lot faster than ordinary cars. NASCAR racers have a top speed of about 340 kilometres per hour.

A NASCAR racing car is more than four times as powerful as a family car.

FACTFILE

Formula 1 racing car

- Engine: 2.4 litres V8
- Power: 740 horsepower
- Top speed: 380 kilometres per hour

HOW FAST?

A Formula 1, IndyCar or NASCAR racing car can travel the length of a football field in 1 second.

Supercars

A few of the cars that are built for driving on public roads can now go faster than the record-breaking cars of the 1920s. These modern marvels are supercars.

The fastest supercar

Supercars are made by some of the greatest names in motoring history, including Ferrari, Bugatti, Jaguar and Lamborghini. The fastest supercar today is the SSC Ultimate Aero TT. Most cars have their engine at the front. The SSC Ultimate Aero TT's **turbocharged** engine is behind the driver. This makes the front of the car lower. Air flows over the car more smoothly and so the car goes faster.

Speed test

On 13 September 2007, the SSC Ultimate Aero TT was tested to prove that it was the fastest supercar. A straight, 19-kilometre long stretch of Highway 221 in the US state of Washington was closed for the test. The car roared down the road at a record speed of 412 kilometres per hour.

The SSC Ultimate Aero TT is made of super-lightweight materials.

The SSC Ultimate Aero TT is very low. It stands just over one metre high.

FACTFILE

SSC Ultimate Aero TT

- Engine: 6.2-litre turbocharged V8
- Power: 1183 horsepower
- Top speed: 412 kilometres per hour
- Driver: Chuck Bigelow

HOW FAST?

The SSC Ultimate Aero TT can move faster than today's racing cars.

On two wheels

The fastest motorcycles look very different from the motorcycles you see every day. They are called streamliners.

Streamliners

Motorcycles built for breaking speed records don't have to turn corners, or fit in with other traffic. They are designed to do just one thing — go as fast as possible in a straight line. They are so **streamlined** they look like a long thin tube on wheels. The rider lies down inside the tube.

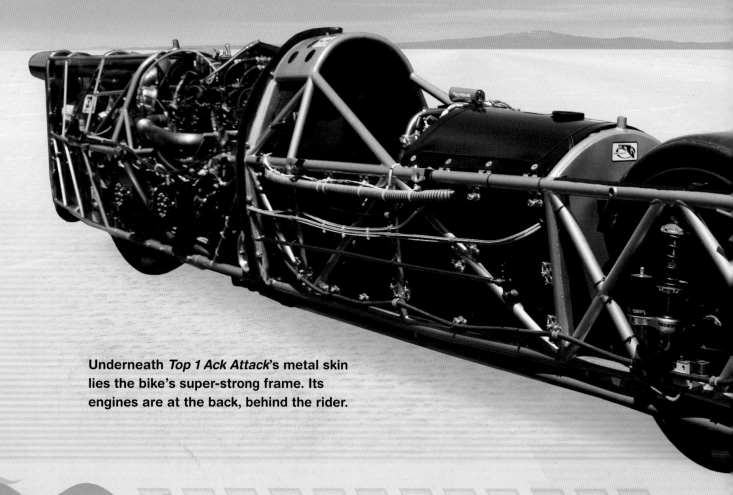

Underneath *Top 1 Ack Attack*'s metal skin lies the bike's super-strong frame. Its engines are at the back, behind the rider.

Top 1 Ack Attack speeds across the Bonneville Salt Flats in the USA.

Top 1 Ack Attack

On 26 September 2008, Rocky Robinson rode his streamliner, called *Top 1 Ack Attack*, to an amazing speed of 580 kilometres per hour. It was faster than any motorcycle had ever gone before. *Top 1 Ack Attack* was so fast because it had two engines working together. Each engine was from a Suzuki Hayabusa, one of the world's fastest motorcycles. Together, they made *Top 1 Ack Attack* unbeatable.

FACTFILE

Top 1 Ack Attack

- Engine: Two Suzuki motorcycle engines
- Power: 800 horsepower
- Top speed: 580 kilometres per hour
- Rider: Rocky Robinson

HOW FAST?

Top 1 Ack Attack went nearly twice as fast as a high-speed train.

Bluebirds

The British racing driver Malcolm Campbell and his son, Donald, set many speed records from the 1920s to the 1960s.

Big engines

When Malcolm Campbell was breaking records, cars were built with bigger and bigger engines to make them go faster. Malcolm Campbell's Bluebird cars had giant engines. In those days, anyone who broke the **land speed record** became famous. Campbell became very famous indeed.

The last Bluebird

Donald Campbell built his own record-breaking car. He called it *Bluebird Proteus CN7*. In 1964, he drove his Bluebird to a new land speed record of 648 kilometres per hour. He had also broken the world water speed record earlier the same year. He is still the only person ever to break the land and water speed records in the same year.

Donald Campbell's Bluebird car had a tall tail to keep it going straight at high speed.

Malcolm Campbell and his son Donald stand by a famous Bluebird car.

FACTFILE

Bluebird Proteus CN7

- Engine: Bristol Siddeley Proteus gas turbine
- Power: 4000 horsepower
- Top speed: 648 kilometres per hour
- Driver: Donald Campbell

HOW FAST?

Bluebird Proteus CN7 travelled twice as fast as a high-speed train goes today.

Spirit of America

In 1963, an American driver called Craig Breedlove surprised everyone by building a car with a jet engine. It looked like a jet plane without wings.

New rules

Record-breaking cars have to follow rules, but there were no rules for **jet-cars**. The rules said that the engine has to drive the car's wheels, but a jet-car's engine doesn't drive the wheels. Instead, the car is pushed along by the jet of air leaving the engine. At first, speed records set by jet-cars were not allowed, but then the rules were changed. Since then, jet-cars have set nearly every land speed record.

Craig Breedlove stands in front of his first jet-car, *Spirit of America*.

Sonic Arrow

Craig Breedlove called his car *Spirit of America*. He drove it at 655 kilometres per hour – faster than any other car in history at that time. He later built another jet-car, *Spirit of America – Sonic 1*. This car went even faster. In 1965, it pushed the record up to 966 kilometres per hour.

Breedlove's second jet-car, *Spirit of America – Sonic 1*, broke the land speed record in 1965.

FACTFILE

Spirit of America – Sonic 1

- Engine: General Electric J79 jet engine
- Power: 17,500 horsepower
- Top speed: 966 kilometres per hour
- Driver: Craig Breedlove

HOW FAST?

Spirit of America – Sonic 1 moved faster than a jet airliner.

Wingfoot Express

After the first Spirit of America broke the land speed record, Tom Green and Walt Arfons built *Wingfoot Express*. This was the next jet-car to break the land speed record.

Air speed

Tom Green was very interested in the way air flows around fast cars. He designed the shape of his new car carefully, so that it would go through the air faster than any other car. Walt Arfons built the car's frame and fitted a jet engine to it. Then Green added the specially designed body.

Wingfoot Express **arrives at the Bonneville Salt Flats, USA.**

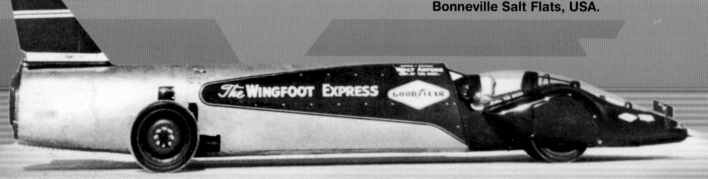

Wingfoot Express's driver sits in front of the car's huge jet engine.

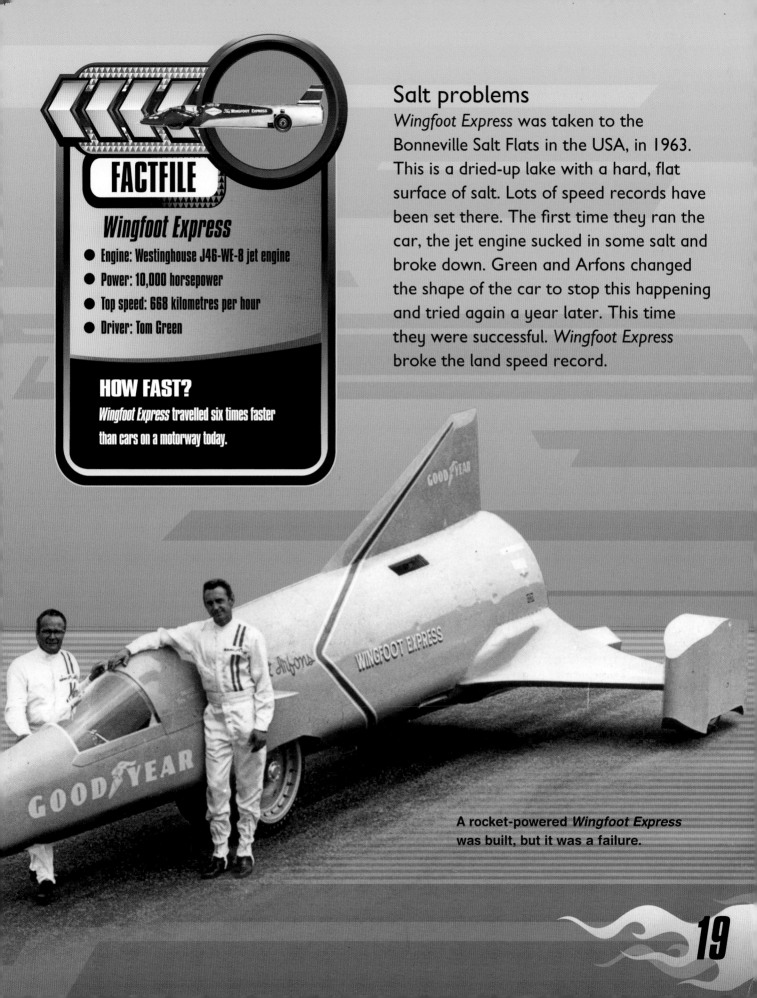

FACTFILE

Wingfoot Express

- Engine: Westinghouse J46-WE-8 jet engine
- Power: 10,000 horsepower
- Top speed: 668 kilometres per hour
- Driver: Tom Green

HOW FAST?

Wingfoot Express travelled six times faster than cars on a motorway today.

Salt problems

Wingfoot Express was taken to the Bonneville Salt Flats in the USA, in 1963. This is a dried-up lake with a hard, flat surface of salt. Lots of speed records have been set there. The first time they ran the car, the jet engine sucked in some salt and broke down. Green and Arfons changed the shape of the car to stop this happening and tried again a year later. This time they were successful. *Wingfoot Express* broke the land speed record.

A rocket-powered *Wingfoot Express* was built, but it was a failure.

19

The Green Monster

Art Arfons, brother of Walt Arfons, built the record-breaking car the *Green Monster*, after he bought himself a jet engine.

The *Green Monster* was powered by a Starfighter jet engine.

Building the monster

The jet engine Art Arfons bought was going cheap, because it was damaged. He repaired the engine and then built a new car around it. He built the car from parts of other cars and trucks. The driver sat in a **cockpit** beside the engine.

The *Green Monster*'s wing held the front of the car down.

Faster and faster

In 1964, Art Arfons showed the world what the *Green Monster* could do. Only three days after *Wingfoot Express* broke the land speed record, the *Green Monster* went even faster. It set a new record of 699 kilometres per hour. It broke the record again in 1965, when it reached 927 kilometres per hour.

FACTFILE

Green Monster

- Engine: General Electric J79 jet engine
- Power: 17,500 horsepower
- Top speed: 927 kilometres per hour
- Driver: Art Arfons

HOW FAST?

The *Green Monster* went about as fast as a jet airliner.

Rocket car

Jets are not the only super-engines that can power a record-breaking car. In 1970, a rocket car smashed the land speed record.

Long and thin

The *Blue Flame* was a **rocket** on wheels. Its long, thin nose held fuel called **liquid natural gas**, or LNG. This was burned by a rocket motor in the car's tail. Instead of taking off like a space rocket, the *Blue Flame* went along the ground very fast indeed.

The *Blue Flame*'s driver, Gary Gabelich, checks out the car.

The *Blue Flame* had a very slim body to go as fast as possible.

The *Blue Flame*'s rocket engine fires amid clouds of smoke.

Driving a rocket

A racing driver called Gary Gabelich was chosen to drive the new rocket car. On 23 October 1970, Gabelich climbed into the car's cockpit, fired the rocket, and drove the *Blue Flame* across the Bonneville Salt Flats to an amazing new land speed record of 1001 kilometres per hour. It was the first time a car had ever set a record faster than 1000 kilometres per hour. *Blue Flame*'s record was not broken for another 13 years.

FACTFILE

Blue Flame

- Engine: RD HP-LNG rocket
- Power: 35,000 horsepower
- Top speed: 1001 kilometres per hour
- Driver: Gary Gabelich

HOW FAST?

A car going as fast as the *Blue Flame* could drive the distance between the North and South poles in less than a day.

Thrust 2

The work to design and build the next successful land speed record car began in England in 1978. The result was a jet-car called *Thrust 2*.

Straight as an arrow

Thrust 2 was built a bit like an arrow. Most of its weight was at the front, like the point of an arrow. **Fins** at the back kept the car going in a straight line, as an arrow's feathers do. The wheels were made by hand from solid metal.

Black Rock

Bad weather in the early 1980s made it impossible to run cars at the Bonneville Salt Flats, where land speed records were usually set. The salty ground was too soft. The Black Rock Desert in Nevada was used instead. On 4 October 1983, with Richard Noble at the controls, *Thrust 2* hurtled across the desert. It set a new record of 1019 kilometres per hour.

FACTFILE

Thrust 2

- Engine: Rolls-Royce Avon jet engine
- Power: 34,000 horsepower
- Top speed: 1019 kilometres per hour
- Driver: Richard Noble

HOW FAST?

Thrust 2 travels 1 kilometre every 3 seconds.

Thrust 2's land speed record was set by British driver Richard Noble.

Thrust 2 made its first low-speed test runs on rubber tyres.

Faster than sound

A British team decided to build the first supersonic car. It was designed to go faster than the speed of sound, but no one knew if that was possible.

Thrust SSC

The team, led by Richard Noble, called their car *Thrust SSC*. Noble had already driven the *Thrust 2* record-breaking car, but this time he decided that he would run the project and someone else would drive the car. The driver he chose was Andy Green.

Thrust SSC's twin jet engines power it across the desert.

Two jet engines

Thrust SSC was massive. It weighed 10 tonnes, or about six or seven times the weight of an ordinary family car. It was powered by two mighty jet engines, side by side. On 15 October 1997, *Thrust SSC* succeeded in setting the first **supersonic** land speed record. This was 50 years and one day after the first supersonic flight by a plane.

Thrust SSC's driver, Andy Green, sits between its two jet engines.

FACTFILE

Thrust SSC

- Engine: Two Rolls-Royce Spey 205 jet engines
- Power: 100,000 horsepower
- Top speed: 1227 kilometres per hour
- Driver: Andy Green

HOW FAST?

Thrust SSC travelled faster on the ground than a jet airliner flies through the air.

27

Future records

Two new cars are being built to try to break speed records in the future. One is an American car called the *North American Eagle*, and the other is a British car called *Bloodhound SSC*.

Here comes Eagle

North American Eagle is a jet-car that is being designed to set a land speed record of about 1300 kilometres per hour. The bright-red car has a nose like a needle, and is powered by an engine from a Starfighter jet fighter plane.

The *North American Eagle* car looks like a fighter plane on wheels.

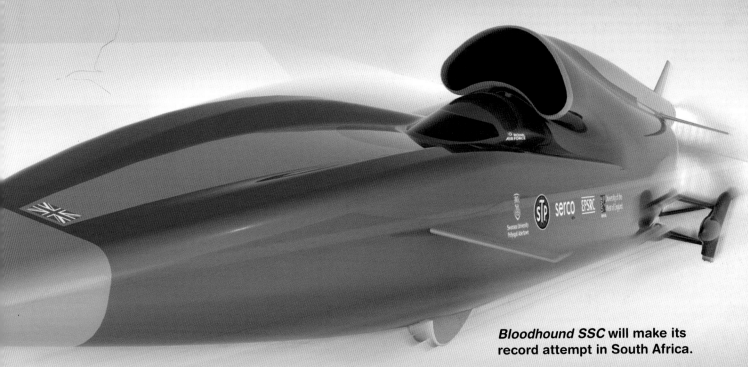

Bloodhound SSC will make its record attempt in South Africa.

Jet and rocket

Bloodhound SSC is aiming at a much faster record. If it goes as fast as its designers think it should, it will be the first car to reach 1600 kilometres per hour. *Bloodhound SSC*'s great speed comes from a jet engine and a rocket. The car will start off by using its jet engine only. When it reaches 480 kilometres per hour, the rocket will fire and boost the car to its amazing top speed.

FACTFILE

Bloodhound SSC

- Engine: A Eurojet EJ200 jet engine and a rocket
- Power: Unknown
- Top speed: 1600 kilometres per hour
- Driver: Andy Green

HOW FAST?
Bloodhound SSC will go as fast as a fighter jet.

Glossary

cockpit The part of a racing car or record-breaking car where the driver sits.

designer A person who creates the shape and plans how something, such as a car, operates.

electric car A car powered by one or more electric motors.

engineer A person who uses scientific knowledge to solve technical problems.

fin A panel or surface that helps to keep a car going steadily in a straight line.

horsepower A measurement of the power of a machine such as a car.

jet-car A car powered by a jet engine instead of by an ordinary car engine. The world's fastest cars are jet-cars.

jet engine An engine that produces a fast stream of hot air. The air is heated by burning fuel with oxygen from the air. The air expands and rushes out of the engine as a jet of hot air.

kilometre A length or distance of 1000 metres.

land speed record The highest speed reached by a car on land.

liquid natural gas (LNG) Gas that comes from under the ground and is then changed into a liquid. LNG can be burned in an engine to produce power.

NASCAR The National Association for Stock Car Auto Racing in the United States.

petrol engine An engine that burns petrol inside it to produce power.

rocket An engine that burns fuel with oxygen to produce a fast jet of hot gas that pushes a vehicle along.

streamlined With a slim, smooth shape designed to go through air very easily, without resistance.

supersonic Faster than the speed of sound. The speed of sound in air depends on how warm or cold the air is.

turbocharged Boosted in power. A turbocharger is a machine that forces extra air into an engine so that it burns more fuel to give extra power.

Notes for parents and teachers

Shape and size

Look through the pictures in the book and talk about the vehicles and why they are different shapes and sizes. Think about how other road vehicles, such as buses and trucks, compare to the vehicles in this book. The fastest record-breaking cars are specially designed to go very fast. Think about how other types of cars are designed for a particular purpose. For example, family cars are comfortable, with space for passengers and bags. Talk about why sports cars are smaller than family cars, and why SUVs are taller than racing cars.

Speed limits

Cars set speed records on closed roads, race tracks, airfields and courses specially set up for record-breaking. Talk about why speed records are set in places where there is no other traffic. Drivers are not allowed to go as fast as they like on public roads. Talk about the reasons for speed limits and why there are different speed limits on different roads.

Danger of speed

Driving a car very fast is dangerous. Talk about how the drivers of very fast cars try to stay safe by wearing a seatbelt, a helmet and fireproof clothes.

Materials

Cars are made from different materials. Think about why a car's body is made of steel, the windows from glass and the tyres from rubber. Why do you think the fastest cars are made of lighter materials like carbon fibre and titanium?

Drawing

Make a drawing of your own record-breaking car. What would it look like? What shape would it be? What would it be made of? What sort of engine would it have? Where would it go to set its speed records? How fast do you think it would go?

Controls

Discuss the ways in which a driver controls a car – a steering wheel to steer the car, an accelerator pedal or thrust lever to go faster, and brakes to slow down. The fastest cars have parachutes to slow them down until the driver can use the brakes.

Index